The Invisible Lion

Your 28-Day Recovery Plan

Printed in the United Kingdom

www.theinvisiblelion.com

First Edition, October 2020

979-8693761209

Independently published

CONTENTS

INTRODUCTION

Imagine you are walking along, minding your own business, when across the road you see a man running. He's waving his arms wildly, screaming, turning this way and that, looking over his shoulder. He's dishevelled. He seems feral, wild. He's frightening.

People get out of his way. They avoid him, crossing the road as they see him coming. You feel the urge to do the same because this guy makes you feel really uncomfortable. You tell yourself that he is crazy, that you are not like him.

You are just about to look the other way when you see something.

Around the corner bounds a lion. A fully grown, roaring lion. And it's running after the man. Suddenly, you see the man differently. You understand that he is in danger. You want to help him. You are not alone. Other people see the danger. They also want to help.

No one thinks the man is crazy anymore. They are no longer afraid of him.

The man has not changed. He is still running wildly,

terrified, blind with panic. Yet everything else has changed. His behaviour is exactly the same as before. His body is doing exactly what it was doing before. And somehow he has gone from crazy to normal, from being avoided to being helped.

What if you are the same? What if everything you think is wrong with you is actually normal, but just belongs to a different context? What if you are not crazy, or difficult, or sick, but just can't see the lion?

This book is the companion volume to The Invisible Lion. Together these books will help you to recover regulation in your nervous system, so that you can stop running away from your own invisible lions.

YOUR 28-DAY RECOVERY PLAN

The good news about the 28-Day Plan is that you don't have to do much work. Fifteen to twenty minutes a day should be enough, and you get weekends off!

The goal is to build up some basic skills. You are not trying to become a nervous system superhero overnight. I want you to change a little over time, and then to keep going because, oddly enough, change is also a threat to us. If you take it slowly, you won't freak your nervous system out. Do it a little, but often, so that you don't get overwhelmed.

We are very attached to our existing reactions, realities, personalities and characters. So digging into them and moving them about is not without some peril. But don't worry. If you take it slow, don't expect too much of yourself and are consistent in your practice, you'll start to be okay with the improvements in many areas of your life.

For much of this 28-day plan you will need to have a notebook. There are written exercises, which you could write here if you are reading this in a paperback, but I suggest that you do that in a separate, private journal where you have more space too. I will leave a line or two to make it clear when you should be writing. Or you can buy The Invisible Lion Workbook and do it there; or download a printable version with space for the exercises from www.theinvisiblelion.com

My advice is to start on a Monday. If you miss a day, try to make it up. And if you miss many days, don't worry too much. Just try to pick up where you left off. Your body has its own intelligence and it will all take the time it takes. There is no way to do this wrong.

Your way is the right way.

Week One
Learning

This first week, you are going to revise the basic theory of this book, so that you can apply it to the next three weeks. Each day, you'll have a section to re-visit and then you'll test your knowledge with ten multiple choice questions. I really recommend doing the reading before you do the questions. But if you get a question wrong, just go back to the suggested pages and review the information you missed.

I know it's a bit reminiscent of school tests, but this is important and once you get it, hopefully you'll know it for life. We just need to get your thinking, human brain to agree to help the nervous system. Then we can do what comes next.

You can take the test online if you want. Just go to www.theinvisiblelion.com. Otherwise you'll find the tests for each section here in this book. I'm not going to tell you where the answers are, but if you are determined you will find them!

Week One, Day One
Revision

Today you're going to recap from the beginning. Of time! Remember what you learned about evolution? I want you to revise that Chapters One and Two, recalling how we got from a gazelle's ideal nervous system to a human's interrupted response to threat.

Week One, Day One
Test your knowledge

Take the test!

Question 1: What is natural selection?

A. When you chose a bigger kid to be on your team
B. The process by which some animals survive in the wild and some don't
C. How animals decide which children to keep
D. The reason we vote for our politicians
E. Gene selection by natural disaster

Question 2: Why would a jawless fish want to freeze?

A. Because they are cold
B. To hibernate for the winter
C. So that they avoid other fish
D. To be invisible to predators who are looking for movement
E. They don't like warm water

Question 3: How many brains do I have?

A. It depends on my level of education
B. One but it is not always being used
C. Three, one from the each of the mammal, reptile and human
D. One collective universal brain for the whole planet
E. Just the one above my neck

Question 4: What is a social engagement system?

A. It is the source code of social media
B. It is how PTA committees are organised
C. It tells mammals whom to mate with
D. We use it for paperless invitations to parties
E. It is the branch of the nervous system, which makes us engage with each other

Question 5: In which order would I respond to a threat?

A. Social Engagement System, Vigilance, Fight-or-Flight, Freeze, Death
B. Vigilance, Social Engagement System, Freeze, Fight-or-Flight, Death
C. Freeze, Fight-or-Flight, Vigilance, Social Engagement System, Death
D. Fight-or-Flight, Freeze, Social Engagement System, Vigilance, Death
E. Death, Freeze, Fight-or-Flight, Vigilance, Social Engagement System

Week One, Day One
Test your knowledge

Question 6: What does activation mean?

A. Getting the software to work in your brain
B. Making friends with someone at the gym
C. Getting excited about things that might go wrong
D. Stimulation in the nervous system's accelerator
E. Swiping right on Tinder

Question 7: What is the relationship between activation and a charge in the nervous system?

A. Activation builds up a charge in the nervous system, like acceleration builds up speed
B. You can activate the nervous system without creating any charge
C. Charge and activation are not related
D. Charge and activation are the same thing
E. There is no charge for activation

Question 8: When an activated system freezes, what happens to its charge?

A. It disappears into the body and leeks away
B. It is not known, and it is never seen again
C. It makes the nervous system vibrate at a high speed
D. It is stored in the nervous system in a dormant state
E. It is refunded to the same credit card which paid for it

Question 9: When does a nervous system discharge its frozen activation?

A. Never
B. Whenever it wants to
C. When it is safe enough to resume its organic response to threat
D. When it is told to by the human brain
E. On the first anniversary of freezing

Question 10: What does the human quality of self-awareness do to the process of discharging activation from the nervous system?

A. It makes it much quicker
B. It makes it much slower
C. It doesn't make any difference at all
D. It introduces a parallel dimension to the nervous system activation
E. It observes a threat response with no threat, and, therefore, stops it

Week One, Day Two
Revision

Today is all about the consequences of interrupting the natural threat cycle. This is in Chapters Three, Four and Five. Remind yourself of how a nervous system becomes dysregulated, and how this messes with so much of what we think of as our health.

Week One, Day Two
Test your knowledge

Take the test!

Question 1: What happens if you meet a second lion before you have discharged the threat of the first one?

A. There is no time to return to the set point before being activated again
B. You should run for your life from both of them
C. It depends on if they are related or not
D. Nothing because it makes no difference
E. You won't notice because you are still running away from the first one

Question 2: When we are dysregulated, how does our sense of reality change?

A. We start to think that reading self-help books is more important
B. We see lions where they are not really there in the present moment
C. We become less aware of what is going on around us
D. People are easier to get along with and annoy us less
E. We become more gazelle-like and want to go on safari

Question 3: The difference between an internal and an external threat is?

A. There is no difference because danger is always a threat
B. One you get by email, and the other by messenger
C. An internal threat comes from our thoughts, unlike real external dangers
D. People don't know the difference because they feel the same
E. Only street magicians know the difference

Question 4: We know that someone has experienced a trauma because…?

A. They have told us a shocking story
B. A psychiatrist has diagnosed them with PTSD
C. Why else would they behave so crazily
D. All of their friends agree that their life has been traumatic
E. Their nervous system has not yet recovered to its set point

Question 5: Yoga and meditation are related to the nervous system because…?

A. Everyone does it these days, so it must be important
B. You get really nervous if you don't do these things at least once a day
C. They were the first forms of medicine, so they must be important to mammals
D. They quieten the human brain and let the reptile and mammal brains take over, allowing the body to heal itself
E. Nobody knows, except for the ancient mystics

Week One, Day Two
Test your knowledge

Question 6: Historically, healthcare has been thought of in these different categories?

A. Insured, uninsured and charity cases
B. Mental health and physical health
C. Mind, body and spirit
D. Treatable, untreatable and inexplicable
E. For profit and not for profit

Question 7: Medically unexplained symptoms are…?

A. Something your doctor has confused you about
B. A way to stay off work sick, without having to tell your boss why
C. When everyone knows what's wrong with you, except you
D. Nothing to worry about
E. Diagnoses which do not explain how the problem is caused

Question 8: When I say 'mental health' what is a 'mind'?

A. Only a philosopher can answer this question
B. The opposite of a body
C. Everything inside your brain
D. Nobody knows and you can't see it or touch it
E. A helpful classification of scientific phenomena

Question 9: A diagnosis in capital letters, like from the DSM 5, is an explanation because…?

A. It tells you what your doctor knows
B It isn't an explanation
C. It brings together all the available evidence base into a diagnosis
D. Academics and doctors have validated these classifications
E. It is not just made up from what you've already said

Question 10: Mental and behavioural health problems, like addiction, are…?

A Just medically unexplained symptoms
B. Healthcare problems equivalent to infection or cancer
C. Ways in which our bodies explore how to heal
D. Usually, examples of deficiencies in our personalities
E. Not interesting to scientist and academics

Week One, Day Three Revision

Today's re-cap is about behaviour. Understanding this is a vital part of our day-to-day recovery. Re-visit Chapters Six and Seven to remind yourself of how dysregulation starts to show up in everyday life, through the ways that we behave and how that affects our relationships.

Week One, Day Three
Test your knowledge

Take the test!

Question 1: Triggers and Baggage work with each other in which of the following ways?

A. You can carry your triggers more easily in your baggage
B. They are independent of each other
C. Baggage can cause triggers to turn up in the real world
D. They are just different names for the same thing
E. Triggers set off the stored energy in your baggage

Question 2: The three types of reactions to triggers have what relationship with evolution?

A. Each of them evolves over time
B. They were started in the Garden of Eden
C. They are not related to evolution
D. Each fits a different layer of evolved response to threat
E. There is only one type of reaction to a trigger

Question 3: Boundaries are used in which of these ways?

A. To measure the distance between me and another nervous system
B. To explain to me what is okay for me so I can manage it
C. To get other people to do what I need, so that I can feel safe
D. For exerting influence and pressure over people who are rude
E. To make me easier to live with at work and home

Question 4: Containment is done in which of these ways?

A. By not using the word "you", and by also speaking up
B. Making sure that you don't say what you are thinking
C. Doing and saying nothing until much later
D. Putting everything you are thinking and feeling in a box
E. Spraying your thoughts and feelings around for others to hold

Question 5: Boundaries and containment combined are useful because…?

A. They help you to control other people's behaviour
B. They are the same thing
C. It creates a bubble of safety around the nervous system in which it can heal
D. They are not useful to combine because they contradict each other
E. This is all you need to be happy

Week One, Day Three
Test your knowledge

Question 6: Stabilising our behaviour stabilises the nervous system because…?

A. We annoy people less
B. Our mammal is nicer to other mammals, and this helps the mammal brain
C. Stable nervous systems create stable behaviour
D. It doesn't work like that and they are unrelated
E. When we protect our nervous system, it can act as if it is more regulated

Question 7: When an over-reaction has a relationship with an over-reaction, what happens?

A. Both of them increasingly trigger each other and they move apart
B. They hold each other comfortably in a balanced way
C. One dominates the other who becomes frozen and stuck
D. Sometimes it works, and sometimes it doesn't
E. True love is possible, but not guaranteed

Question 8: When an over-reaction has a relationship with an under-reaction what happens?

A. Both of them increasingly trigger each other and they move apart
B. They hold each other comfortably in a balanced way
C. One dominates the other who becomes frozen and stuck
D. Sometimes it works, and sometimes it doesn't
E. True love is possible, but not guaranteed

Question 9: How do we know the difference between a Goldilocks nervous system in a relationship, and one with just good boundaries and containment?

A. There are just different ways of saying the same thing
B. There is no difference, other than the internal experience of the latter
C. The Goldilocks nervous system looks like it works much better
D. You can't compare them, like apples and oranges
E. The Goldilocks nervous system is just a fairy tale

Question 10: Why do we choose the people we do to have relationships with?

A. Because of our chemistry
B. We don't choose, them they choose us
C. Our nervous systems fall in love with their nervous systems
D. Their triggers match our frozen baggage, which gives it a chance to activate
E. Mammals will be mammals

Week One, Day Four
Revision

Today, we look at love, particularly our first attempts at loving the people who raised us, what we learned from them about love and our own attempts to find loving relationships in life. This is in Chapters Eight and Nine.

Week One, Day Four
Test your knowledge

Take the test!

Question 1: Babies are born with which kind of a nervous system?

A. They don't yet have a nervous system
B. All kinds of different nervous systems, depending on their parents
C. Their nervous systems look like they are dysregulated
D. They only get nervous when their mothers are not present
E. Parents can choose their babies' nervous systems when they are born

Question 2: Attachment styles are formed by early relationships because…?

A. There is no other time to form them
B. Babies and young children tend to copy their primary caregivers' regulation
C. Most people screw up their children, and start doing that from birth
D. They are just as likely to be formed in later relationships
E. Attachment styles change all the time, however old you are

Question 3: An over-reacting early caregiver will lead to which problem?

A. It leads to a resistant attachment style in the child
B The child will not be affected by this kind of behaviour
C. It's impossible to tell because every family is different
D. It leads to an avoidant attachment style in the child
E. The child will not form any relationships

Question 4: An under-reacting early care giver will lead to which problem?

A. It leads to a resistant attachment style in the child
B. The child will not be affected by this kind of behaviour
C. It's impossible to tell because every family is different
D. It leads to an avoidant attachment style in the child
E. The child will not form any relationships

Question 5: You can help people to recover from an attachment problem at any age by…?

A. Explaining to them everything in this book
B. Telling them to change their behaviour and find new relationships
C. You can't recover from an attachment problem
D. It can only be done in childhood, by changing their parent's behaviours
E. Having a relationship with them with boundaries and containment

Week One, Day Four
Test your knowledge

Question 6: A love addict comes from which kind of a nervous system?

A. Love isn't related to the nervous system
B. An over-reacting nervous system
C. Anyone can be addicted to love
D. An under-reacting nervous system
E. It can come from any kind of a nervous system

Question 7: A love avoidant comes from which kind of a nervous system?

A. Love isn't related to the nervous system
B. An over-reacting nervous system
C. Anyone can avoid love
D. An under-reacting nervous system
E. It can come from any kind of a nervous system

Question 8: I can be a love addict and a love avoidant at the same time if…?

A. Anyone can be if they have experienced both kinds of attachment in childhood
B. You are either always one or always the other, and you can't swap
C. Everyone is always one or the other but never both
D. You can't be one without the other if you are in love
E. Most people are very unlikely to be either, ever, so both is almost impossible

Question 9: Romantic relationships are a chance to heal because…?

A. Love makes us feel less triggered and, therefore, we seem better
B. Falling in love is the only way to heal a broken heart
C. If we can use them to activate frozen baggage while staying safe, then we can heal
D. Romantic relationships usually damage us and cannot heal us at all
E. St. Valentine was the patron saint of nervous systems

Question 10: Healthy romantic relationships require…?

A. Two willing participants and a bit of luck
B. Love conquers all and solves all problems
C. All romantic relationships are unhealthy, even if they are fun
D. Weapons-grade boundaries and containment
E. An ability to keep secrets, and the willingness to lie frequently

Week One, Day Five
Revision

On the last day of Week One, we bring it all together. Today, I'm asking you to look at the more complicated effects of dysregulation on personality and character, and how this has affected our whole world. This is all in Chapter Ten.

Week One, Day Five
Test your knowledge

Take the test!

Question 1: Which combination of child, teen and adult can I be?

A. Child, teen, adult, or any two, or any three, all at the same time
B. I can be a child or a teen or an adult
C. I can be either an adult, or a teen or a child
D. It is only possible to be one person at a time
E. It depends how old I am

Question 2: Why do I have a hung parliament in my brain, and who is in charge?

A. Your politics are often very confused, and it's not clear who is president
B. My brain is not a hung parliament, and is very clear about its choices
C. Sometimes I'm a bit confused about life, but I sort myself out in the end
D. It's not possible to generalise because every brain is different
E. The brain has many decision-making centres, and one of them eventually wins

Question 3: What other responses can I have to threat after social engagement other than fight, flight or freeze?

A. There are no other choices because these are the only evolved responses
B. You can become vigilant before a reaction, and have active and passive freeze states
C. You can simply deal with it without having to get so worked up
D. You can simultaneously deploy a mixture of all three
E. You don't have to respond to threat at all if you are at peace with yourself

Question 4: What possible nervous system explanation could I give for dissociation?

A. If I can't decide which attachment style I like best, I dissociate
B. Dissociation is not related to the nervous system
C. It is when the brain can't resolve the fragmented coalition government
D. Dissociation is just another mammalian response to threat
E. Nobody knows what dissociation is

Question 5: How many personalities do I have, and which is me?

A. You are always the same person, just with different moods
B. You might be different people in different relationships to suit your partner
C. Everyone has multiple personalities they are unaware of
D. Depending on your regulation and reactions, you can have different personalities
E. It's not a relevant question for the nervous system

Week One, Day Five
Test your knowledge

Question 6: Which character strategies am I born with, and are any of them actually me?

A. A strategy is an adaptation to your dysregulation style and therefore not really you
B. You are always born with a dominant character strategy that defines you
C. You can have any that you like and each is an aspect of your true self
D. They don't really exist and are just ideas psychologists use
E. You are born with all of them and use them when you need to

Question 7: Our world is affected by our individual nervous systems in which ways?

A. It makes very little difference, other than to our sense of self
B. Each person is greatly affected, but the effects cancel out over larger populations
C. The environment suffers from our lack of safety but our health is not affected
D. All people, relationships, families, communities, countries and the planet are affected
E. Nothing really matters because it is all going to be okay in the end

Question 8: What are the theoretical steps required to get back to an ideal state of regulation?

A. There is nothing you can do to get to an ideal state of regulation
B. Only by meditating up a mountain for many years can regulation be recovered
C. In theory, discharging all the responses to all threats will restore regulation
D. As long as you are having fun in your life, personal regulation is unnecessary
E. Scientists are working on equipment to do this for you

Question 9: What are the practical steps I could take on my own to get better-regulated?

A. Getting a friend to treat you better will start to make you feel more regulated
B. I need to not be in a relationship and to start to love myself instead
C. There is nothing I can do but others can do it for me
D. Just deciding to start to be regulated is enough; the body will follow
E. Recovery starts with stabilisation from changing your own behaviour and boundaries

Question 10: When I am going to do the rest of this 28-day plan?

A. Sometime
B. Maybe
C. Now
D. Never
E. There's a plan?

Week One, Day Six
Review

It's the weekend. Relax. You don't need to do anything today, but if you want to, you can look back over the questions and your answers in this section, picking out the things you found difficult or confusing. You could even talk to a friend about it and see if another perspective helps.

If not, let it go. It will all make sense in the end when it is supposed to. Don't worry if you can't get it all straight, right away.

Week One, Day Seven
Rest

Seriously. Rest. It's the seventh day.

Week Two
Reframing

So, you've read the instructions in Book Four. We spent a lot of time there, looking at how to reframe our experience of life through the lens of our model of trigger, baggage and reaction.

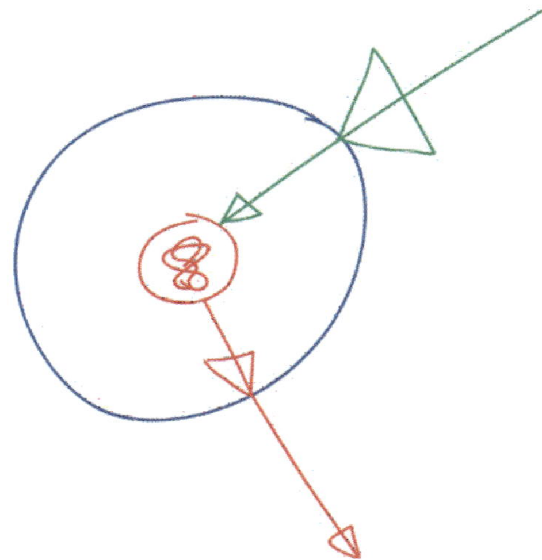

Sometimes, it can be tricky. The key to success here is to keep it simple and to keep it about yourself. To do that, we are going to use a formula to break down our communication, and the first person you are going to be talking to is yourself.

Each day this week, I invite you to start with thinking of three times that you were triggered in life. This could be from a time ten minutes ago or fifty years ago. You just need to find some material to practice with. You will take the first three examples that come into your head and write them down as brief headlines of the events. Then you will rank them from one, to three, in order of importance to you. We are going to work on the top one to reframe this experience.

You just have to think about the headline, and then follow the instructions. It should be quite easy.

Again, there is no right answer you're aiming for, but if you find yourself trying to point fingers at someone else, that's a red flag, showing you that you need to come back to what's going on for you in the diagram above.

Once you have your reframe, we are going to prepare for finding a boundary for this trigger that works for you.

And that's a good day's work. If you follow the script, you can't go too far wrong.

Week Two, Day One

Take a moment. Give yourself some space and peace. Put the phone on airplane mode or turn off the Wi-Fi if you have to.

Try to settle a bit on what is going on inside your mind and body. Now go and look for trouble. Where inside of you is there a ripple of discomfort, discontent or distress?

Left to its own devices, that ripple will turn into a thought, often a memory and usually about someone else. Write down a short headline about this thought, memory or person.

Headline 1 ______________________________

____

____

Do it again, looking for another trigger to work on. Take your time. Try to settle a bit on what is going on inside your mind and body.

Somewhere inside you there is a ripple of discomfort. Let it become a thought or a memory. Write down a short headline about it.

Headline 2 ______________________________

____

____

One more time. Find the ripple. Let it become a thought or a memory. Write it down.

Headline 3 ______________________________

____

____

Well done!

You now have three headlines for historical events that live on in your nervous system.

Let's pick one to work on.

Week Two, Day One

Imagine you are the editor of a newspaper, and, at your morning editorial meeting, three of your best writers come to you with these three stories. You can only have one headline on your front page. Which one do you want to work on?

Pick the story you think has the most widespread appeal. You want people to read your paper. You want stories that translate to the largest possible audience. You want to cover things that feel important. Ask yourself, which of these three headlines feels most important to you?

Now you are going to do the reframe exercise on this story. Don't try to do this if you haven't read Part Four. And don't read Part Four if you haven't read parts One to Three! You need to know why you are doing this more than you need to know how to do it.

Write down the headline again ______________________________

____

Now find the trigger that began this story. You are like a film director writing your script to recreate the event. Just recall what you saw and what you heard. Actions and sounds. That's all.

I noticed this trigger.

What I saw was ______________________________

____

One more time. Find the ripple. Let it become a thought or a memory. Write it down.

What I heard was ______________________________

____

It doesn't need to be longer than this. Sometimes, it's tempting to use this as a way to attack someone else's behaviour but try to resist that temptation. Keep it really simple and about you.

Next, I want you to write down your reaction. This can be more complicated, but again, let's aim to make it really simple. Record what you remember or noticed about your sensations, emotions and thoughts. Crucially, you only want to focus on thoughts about yourself, not others.

I noticed this reaction.

I became aware of these sensations in my body ______________________________

____

I became aware of these emotions happening ____________________

____

____

I became aware of these thoughts about myself ____________________

____

____

Now you're ready to have a quick guess at the baggage. Go with what comes to mind immediately after writing out the trigger and the reaction. Don't dwell on it. There is no right answer. Just fill in the gap below.

When I look at this trigger and reaction something about it feels familiar

____

____

____

If nothing about it feels familiar, that's fine. Just let it go. It might come to you later.

This might feel a bit difficult the first time you do it. And you might feel like you are not getting anywhere, or that it doesn't work. Don't worry; that's very normal. This is a skill that you will build with practice. And practice is what this week is for.

So, have another go tomorrow.

Week Two, Day One
Boundary Prep

You can now use this story to prepare for setting your own boundaries around this issue. Go back to your main headline.

Write down the headline again____

____

____

Write down even more simply what triggered it.

What I saw was ____

____

____

What I heard was____

____

____

How would you need that to be different, if you were not going to be triggered by it? You can usually find out by asking yourself, "What was okay for me" and "What wasn't okay for me".

It doesn't feel okay for me when ____

____

____

Now you have some helpful knowledge. You know what the problem was.

In the future, you can try to make what's not okay for you happen less. That's your job. No one else's. We will do that in more detail in Week Four. But that's enough work for today. You now know what happened, where the trigger might have come from, and what you would like to be different in the future to make it less difficult.

Think about how this story now reads in your newspaper. How very different is that to the story you might have written if you had not done this exercise? It is this difference which gives you the opportunity to begin to make a real, lasting transformational change in your life.

Week Two, Day Two
Three Times I was Triggered

Today, we'll do the same exercises again, delving into any new stories that you sense you'd like to work on. Take a moment.

Try to settle a bit on what is going on inside your mind and body. Now go and look for trouble. Where inside of you is there a ripple of discomfort, discontent or distress?

Left to its own devices, that ripple will turn into a thought, often a memory and usually about someone else. Write down a short headline about this thought, memory or person.

Headline 1 ____

____

____

Do it again, looking for another trigger to work on. Take your time. Try to settle a bit on what is going on inside your mind and body.

Somewhere inside you there is a ripple of discomfort. Let it become a thought or a memory. Write down a short headline about it.

Headline 2 ____

____

____

One more time. Find the ripple. Let it become a thought or a memory. Write it down.

Headline 3 ____

____

____

Well done! You now have three headlines for historical events that live on in your nervous system. Let's pick one to work on.

Week Two, Day Two
Reframing

Imagine you are the editor of a newspaper and pick the story which you want to be the headline of your paper. Ask yourself, "Which of these three stories feels most important to my life".

Write down the headline again ____

____

____

Now find the trigger that began this story. Remember that you are like a film director, writing your script to recreate the event. Just recall what you saw and what you heard.

I noticed this trigger.

What I saw was ____

____

____

What I heard was ____

____

____

Remember to keep it simple and short. Next, you're going to write down your reaction. Again, make it really simple and about you, not others. All you need is what you remember or noticed about your sensations, emotions and thoughts.

I noticed this reaction.

I became aware of these sensations in my body____________________________

____

____

I became aware of these emotions happening ____________________________

____

____

I became aware of these thoughts about myself ___________________________

____

____

Now have a quick guess at the baggage. What comes to mind immediately after writing out the trigger and the reaction? Fill in the gap below without overthinking it.

When I look at this trigger and reaction something about it feels familiar ______________

____

____

Well done! Just like yesterday, you have one more task to complete.

Week Two, Day Two
Boundary Prep

Go back to your main headline.

Write down the headline again ______________________________

____

____

Write down again, even more simply, what triggered it.

What I saw was ______________________________

____

____

What I heard was ______________________________

____

____

How would you need that to be different if you were not going to be triggered by it? You can usually find out by thinking about what is okay for you and what is not okay for you.

It doesn't feel okay for me when ______________________________

____

____

You've now done your work for today.

Week Two, Day Three
Three Times I was Triggered

Today, we're looking for three more headlines. Find a ripple and write down short headline about the thoughts, memories or people that come to mind.

Headline 1 ______________________________

____

____

And again. Find the ripple. Let it become a thought or a memory. Write it down.

Headline 2 ______________________________

____

____

One more time. Find the ripple. Let it become a thought or a memory. Write it down.

Headline 3 ______________________________

____

____

Week Two, Day Three
Reframing

Ready, editor? Pick the headlines that feel most important to you right now.

Write down the headline again ______________________________

____

____

To find the trigger that began this story, write down what you saw and what you heard.

I noticed this trigger.

What I saw was ______________________________

____

____

What I heard was ______________________________

____

____

Keep it brief and simple.

Now let's recall what happened next. I noticed this reaction.

I became aware of these sensations in my body ______________________

____

____

I became aware of these emotions happening ______________________

____

____

I became aware of these thoughts about myself ______________________

____

____

Try a quick guess at the baggage; this might be feeling like a more intuitive process by now. What comes to mind?

When I look at this trigger and reaction something about it feels familiar ______________

____

____

Nearly there.

Week Two, Day Three
Boundary Prep

Choose your main headline.

Write down the headline again ______________________________

____

____

Write down again even more simply, what triggered it.

What I saw was ______________________________

____

____

What I heard was ______________________________

____

____

How would you need that to be different, if you were not going to be triggered by it? Think about what is okay for you and what is not okay for you.

It doesn't feel okay for me when ______________________________

____

____

That's enough for today.

Week Two, Day Four
Three Times I was Triggered

I hope this is feeling less strange by now. Today is just the same as the other days this week, building on the work you've already done. Let's find three new stories that your body is asking you to look at.

Find a ripple, and write down short headline about the thoughts, memories or people that come to mind.

Headline 1 ______________________________

____

____

And again. Find the ripple. Let it become a thought or a memory. Write it down.

Headline 2 ______________________________

____

____

One more time. Find the ripple. Let it become a thought or a memory. Write it down.

Headline 3 ______________________________

____

____

Week Two, Day Four
Reframing

Which of these three headlines feels most important to your life?

Write down the headline again ______________________________

____

____

To find the trigger, write down what you saw and what you heard.

I noticed this trigger.

What I saw was ______________________________

____

____

What I heard was ______________________________

____

____

Don't be tempted to use this as a way to attack someone else's behaviour. Keep it really simple and about you.

What was your reaction? What do you remember or notice about your sensations, emotions and thoughts?

I noticed this reaction.

I became aware of these sensations in my body ______________________________

____

____

I became aware of these emotions happening ______________________________

____

____

I became aware of these thoughts about myself ______________________________

____

____

Now have a quick guess at the baggage.

When I look at this trigger and reaction something about it feels familiar____________________

____

____

And, as you'll know by now, you have one more task to complete.

Week Two, Day Four
Boundary Prep

Go to your main headline and write it down again ______________________________

____

____

Write down again even more simply, what triggered it.

What I saw was ____

____

____

What I heard was ____

____

____

What would need to be different, if you were not going to be triggered by it? Let's explore what's okay and not okay in that context.

It doesn't feel okay for me when ______________________________________

____

____

And that's Day Four wrapped up.

Week Two, Day Five
Three Times I was Triggered

This is the last day you'll need to dig into those experiences that are causing any kind of discomfort, discontent or stress. You're probably quite good at this by now.

Find a ripple and write down short headline about the thoughts, memories or people that come to mind.

Headline 1 ____

____

____

And again. Find the ripple. Let it become a thought or a memory. Write it down.

Headline 2 ____

____

____

One more time. Find the ripple. Let it become a thought or a memory. Write it down.

Headline 3 ____

____

____

Week Two, Day Five
Reframing

Which of these three headlines feels most important to your life?

Write down the headline again ______________________________

____

____

To find the trigger, write down what you saw and what you heard.

I noticed this trigger.

What I saw was ______________________________

____

____

What I heard was ______________________________

____

____

Don't be tempted to use this as a way to attack someone else's behaviour. Keep it really simple and about you.

What was your reaction? What do you remember or notice about your sensations, emotions and thoughts?

I noticed this reaction.

I became aware of these sensations in my body ______________________________

____

____

I became aware of these emotions happening ______________________________

____

____

I became aware of these thoughts about myself ______________________________

____

____

Now have a quick guess at the baggage. Just fill in the gap below with whatever comes to mind.

When I look at this trigger and reaction something about it feels familiar _______________

____

____

Well done! The last step now is prepare for boundary work.

Week Two, Day Five
Boundary Prep

Go to your main headline, and write it down again ____________________

____

____

Write down again even more simply, what triggered it.

What I saw was ____________________

____

____

What I heard was ____________________

____

____

What needs to be different so that you are not going to be triggered by it in future? Think about what is okay for you, and what is not okay for you.

It doesn't feel okay for me when ____________________

____

____

That's it! You've got through the week.

Week Two, Day Six
Review

You've done a lot of work this week, which, I hope, got a little easier each day. The more you practice this, the better you get at it. If you did this every day for the rest of your life, it would do you no harm at all.

Eventually, you might be able to do it all the time, live, in every situation as it happens. That would completely change how you view your life and how you experience it.

So, today, you only need to have a look back at what you have written this week, reviewing it more as a witness than a participant. See what you notice. Things might look a bit different from the outside, looking in. You might notice where your language was a bit spikey or where you were really talking about someone else, rather than your own experience. These are your opportunities to clean things up a bit.

Just noticing how things can seem different when you are not caught up in the energy of them is a big step. Re-write anything you read if you think you want to make it better. The goal is to get to the point where you are watching your nervous system and describing it, rather than just bring trapped in it and reacting to it.

Week Two, Day Seven
Rest

Rest. That's all.

Notes

Week Three
Connecting

Each day last week you worked in some detail to reframe your experience of an event that had triggered you. We are going to take that same important event from each day last week and use it to practice doing some time-traveling.

In each of these examples last week, you found your baggage by reflecting on what felt familiar about your reaction. You may have thought of something very specific, like an actual event, or something more general, like a pattern of events, behaviours or experiences.

This week we are going to move you down your brainstem a bit, away from thoughts, from ideas and even from language, into the body and its experiences.

The reframe was an observation of your nervous system today; a trigger, your reaction and an idea about the baggage behind it. The aim of this section is to link that baggage to something unfinished in your body from the past. This opens up your awareness from the limitations of just today, to the whole timeframe from when the baggage was created, right up until now, represented by the black box in the diagram below.

We do this by becoming a gazelle again, connecting to our inner mammal and leaving behind the problems created by the self-awareness of our thinking, human brain. This allows new connections to be made, and is the gateway into the transformational work of the final week of this plan.

One irony of all of this is that you are, right now, reading a book. Gazelles tend not to read. By reading, you are activating your thinking brain. And I am trying to get you to do the opposite.

So, to get you ready, you are going to learn how to do something called a 'body scan'. I'm going to recommend you do this with a video rather than reading it on the page here. You can search on the internet for body scan videos or find one you like at www.theinvisiblelion.com.

Each day this week, you are going to review the piece of work you did on the corresponding day in Week Two that will be your material for this exercise. You are going to read that story again, put down the book, and then do the body scan exercise while this story is still present for you.

Your goal is to use the body scan to find a place in your body where the sensations match the activation from the baggage of that story. You will, somewhere, somehow, feel it in your body, and that's why the body scan helps you to find it.

Once you find it, you will be able to use that sensation and float it back in time. Sounds weird? It is, a bit. But you can do it by asking your body one simple question:

Can you float that back in time and see where it goes?

Remember, don't ask your brain! Ask your body.

Whatever comes back to you from this question, try to allow it to be whatever it is. It might not make any sense at first. So, don't judge the answer. People often discount the thoughts or memories that come up because they can't understand the connection. Be prepared for that. This is not about logic; this is about allowing the body to make connections through its senses. Don't judge.

Once you settle on an experience or a memory, I want you to shift gear, get out your journal and write down as much about it as possible. You will write about both what you remember and what you notice about your sensations, now, as you remember it. This will then be your material for Week Four.

A word of warning; if you get really good at this, you might go deep enough into the experience that you don't want to wait until Week Four to process it. That's why it might be a good idea, right now, to also read on to Week Four and have those resources ready. If it feels right to you to continue straight from one to the other, then go for it. The body knows best.

On the other hand, it is also more than enough just to do some time-traveling on its own and to write down what that was like for you. That's okay too.

Week Three, Day One
The Body Scan

Review your stories from Day One of Week Two. Find your headline and write it out again. Writing it again is part of the process of getting back into your body.

Write down the headline ____

____

____

Then, read though everything you wrote about it in Week Two until it is something you can hold in mind without looking at the page any more.

Now do the body scan to completion. While it is happening, notice where your body is grabbing your attention. These are the places you want to come back to.

You can search the internet for body scan videos or find one you like at theinvisiblelion.com.

Week Three, Day One
Time-travelling

Once the body scan is finished, ask your body:

Can you float that back in time and see where it goes? and just allow whatever comes up to linger there. Go towards that memory or experience with curiosity. Hang out there for as long as you need to, as you rediscover it. Then, come back to this book.

Now write down in as much detail as you can (in your journal) what you notice about remembering that experience.

This takes me back to ____

____

____

As I rediscover this, I notice the following in my body ____________________

____

____

See, it's quite simple. We will do another one tomorrow.

Week Three, Day Two
The Body Scan

Review your story from Day Two of Week Two.

Write down the headline ______________________________

____

____

Find your headline story, and write it out again. Read through everything you wrote about it in Week Two until it is something you can hold in mind without looking at the page any more.

Then, do the body scan to completion, noticing where your body is grabbing your attention. These are the places you want to come back to.

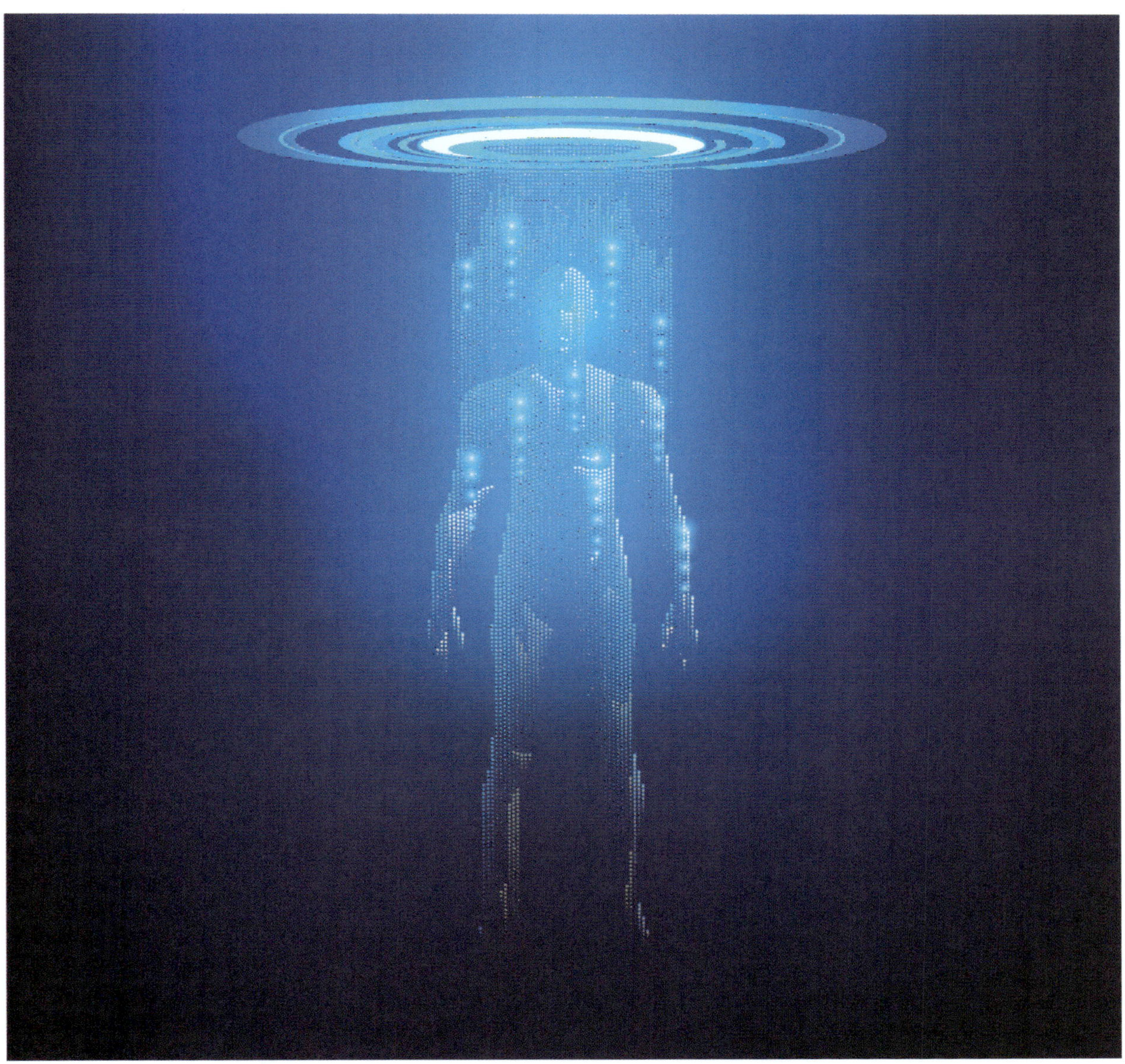

Week Three, Day Two
Time-travelling

Once the body scan is finished, ask your body:

Can you float that back in time and see where it goes? and just allow whatever comes up to linger there. Go towards that memory or experience with curiosity. Hang out there for as long as you need to, as you rediscover it. Then, come back to this book.

Now write down in as much detail as you can (in your journal) what you notice about remembering that experience.

This takes me back to ______________________________

____

____

As I rediscover this, I notice the following in my body ______________________________

____

____

Well done. Keep going tomorrow.

Week Three, Day Three
The Body Scan

Review your stories from Day Three of Week Two.

Write down the headline ____

____

____

Find your headline story, and write it out again. Read through everything you wrote about it in Week Two until it is something you can hold in mind without looking at the page any more. Then, do the body scan to completion, noticing where your body is grabbing your attention. These are the places you want to come back to.

Week Three, Day Three
Time-travelling

Once the body scan is finished, ask your body:

Can you float that back in time and see where it goes? and just allow whatever comes up to linger there. Go towards that memory or experience with curiosity. Hang out there for as long as you need to, as you rediscover it. Then, come back to this book.

Now write down in as much detail as you can (in your journal) what you notice about remembering that experience.

This takes me back to ____

____

____

As I rediscover this, I notice the following in my body ____________________________

____

____

Nice work. Two more to go.

Week Three, Day Four
The Body Scan

Review your stories from Day Four of Week Two.

Write down the headline ______________________________

____

____

Find your headline story, and write it out again. Read through everything you wrote about it in Week Two until it is something you can hold in mind without looking at the page any more.

Then, do the body scan to completion, noticing where your body is grabbing your attention.

These are the places you want to come back to.

Week Three, Day Four
Time-travelling

Once the body scan is finished, ask your body:

Can you float that back in time and see where it goes? and just allow whatever comes up to linger there. Go towards that memory or experience with curiosity. Hang out there for as long as you need to, as you rediscover it. Then, come back to this book.

Now write down in as much detail as you can (in your journal) what you notice about remembering that experience.

This takes me back to ______________________________

____

____

As I rediscover this, I notice the following in my body ______________________________

____

____

Nearly there.

Week Three, Day Five
The Body Scan

Review your stories from Day Five of Week Two.

Write down the headline ____

____

____

Find your headline story, and write it out again. Read though everything you wrote about it in Week Two until it is something you can hold in mind without looking at the page any more.

Then, do the body scan to completion, noticing where your body is grabbing your attention. These are the places you want to come back to.

Week Three, Day Five
Time-travelling

Once the body scan is finished, ask your body:

Can you float that back in time and see where it goes? and just allow whatever comes up to linger there. Go towards that memory or experience with curiosity. Hang out there for as long as you need to, as you rediscover it. Then, come back to this book.

Now write down in as much detail as you can (in your journal) what you notice about remembering that experience.

This takes me back to ______________________________

____

____

As I rediscover this, I notice the following in my body ______________________________

____

____

You made it. That's a good week's work.

Week Three, Day Six
Review

This week, you might have had some great experiences and felt like this is beginning to make sense. Or it may have been very hard, maybe even unproductive. It is important to remember that this is just practice. You are building a skill set day by day, week by week, to allow you to look at your life differently and to experience it with less difficulty.

If you were able to do some time-travelling, have a look at what came up. These are unfinished moments for you, showing you where your unfinished business is. Somewhere around these kinds of experiences, your activation got stuck, so a part of you is still there, always there, waiting to discharge and finish your response to this threat. Next week, I'll show you how to start to do that.

For now, if you were able to get this far on your own, then well done. That shows that your nervous system has resilience and that you are ready to do this work. If you drew a blank, don't worry. Just by understanding what you are trying to do, and by preparing the ground to do it, you are already moving in the right direction.

If you need some help to keep moving from here, a friend or even a relevant professional might be useful to walk through this process with you. We all find safety in different ways and the company of someone we trust is always great for regulating the nervous system, to help to prepare it for completing its unfinished business.

Week Three, Day Seven
Rest

Now let your system rest.

Week Four
Discharging

So far, you have worked hard to create the building blocks for this final piece of work. You have learned the theory and have reframed some of your difficult experiences. You have sensed into the baggage you discovered there and time-travelled back to some earlier experiences which felt the same.

This week, let's see if you can complete some of that unfinished business and discharge some of your baggage. If you can, then you will be less triggered in future and will, therefore, find your boundaries easier to maintain. As a result, containment gets easier, and so, you'll find this work more accessible in general. It gets better and better, once things get moving.

But it's not always easy. It may be that doing this exercise on your own, from a book, is a step too far. And while some people take to it intuitively, others need more preparation, support and time. That's okay. Just do what you can and remember that this book is about creating the discipline of a practice.

Whatever you get out of this week, you will be building the skills to live with your nervous system in a different way. Then, you can see what extra help you might want to make it work for you as well as it possibly can. No one would suggest that everyone's problems can be resolved just by reading the exercises in a book, but some of some people's problems probably can be. And it will be a lot easier to find the right help for everything else, once you know what you are trying to achieve.

So, this week, we are doing this:

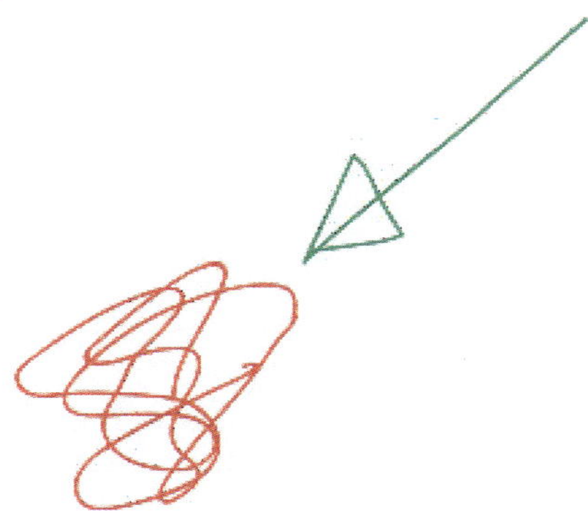

We use the innate wisdom of the body to reconnect with the threat response started by the original lion. Then we let that happen. And, then, we let that happen some more. And we keep going until we feel a sense of something completing.

If we don't get that far, that's okay. This is a beginning and a practice. The first time you meditate or hold a yoga pose or hit a tennis ball, it doesn't usually work very well. That's why you are supposed to practice a little bit every day.

Each day, at the end of this exercise, you'll have a chance to review the whole thing. After reconnecting your body with the original lion, you will be able to see the whole time-line of your problem a bit more clearly. This will help you to set the boundary you need for the future and, even more importantly, to know how you are going to manage that boundary to make sure you keep your nervous system feeling safe.

The safer you feel, the better you will be at this work.

If you get good at this process, the benefits will continue to build in your life. You can then begin to do all four weeks' exercises at once, all in a row, live, in the real world.

Eventually, you will be able to habitually catch yourself being triggered in the moment, reframe the experience, time-travel and discharge the baggage on the spot.

That's the ultimate goal. To become a gazelle again. And if you can do that, while remaining human, not only will you change your life, but you will transform the lives of those around you, your families, communities, societies and the planet.

You really can change the world, one nervous system at a time.

And Ghandi was right; you really do only have to start with you.

Good luck!

Week Four, Day One
Tracking Sensation

Each day this week, we are going to start again with the body scan. This is a really important tool in understanding and regulating your nervous system, so I'm hoping that, over time, it will start to feel very natural to you. Make sure you create a quiet space for yourself to do this work, turning electronics off and settling into the possibility of getting back into your body. You will, by now, have identified your favourite body scan video or audio recording, so try to get into a routine so that it is something familiar to your nervous system. And then begin.

After the body scan, you are going to re-read your time-travel from the corresponding day on Week Three. Try to read it mindfully, slowly, with great care and attention. I want you to get back into the experiences that your body was communicating to you while rediscovering that moment. And this time, we are going to stay with it, to see if anything will move.

So, once you have done the body scan and read the time-travel, it's time to pay attention to your sensations. There are a number of ways to do this. One very simple way do that is to ask yourself a number of questions about the sensations you're aware of, starting with the one which seems most important.

You can ask:
Where is the sensation?
What colour is it?
How big is it?
What shape is it? Round? Jagged? Square?
What textile is it? Smooth? Shiny? Rough?
What temperature is it? Hot? Cold? Warm?

Then, answer these questions in your head. This helps you to pay attention to the sensation, which might be, say, a hot, small, blue, smooth, square egg in the middle of my stomach. And, as you concentrate on this description of it, connecting it to my sensation, ask yourself:

And what happens next?

What you are looking for is whether any of these qualities change. An easy example would be that it gets cooler. Make sure you notice this, by saying to yourself, "It's getting cooler". It's just about noticing the details of the sensation.

Then, ask yourself a very important question:

Can you let that happen?

The correct answer is yes! In some respects, the whole point of reading this book is to bring you to this right answer at this vital point in your recovery. You might remember that the problem started in Box 4, with self-awareness; this moment is the antidote.

Can you let that happen?

Yes!

When you let this happen, you are restarting your interrupted response to the threat of the original lion. Then you keep going, letting it happen until you come to a natural pause in the process.

Then, go back to the questions about the sensation:

Where is it?
What colour is it?
How big is it?
What shape is it? Round? Jagged? Square?
What texture is it? Smooth? Shiny? Rough?
What temperature is it? Hot? Cold? Warm?

Then, ask yourself:
And what happens next?
Then, ask yourself:
Can you let that happen?

And then let it happen.

Keep going until you feel that things have come to a natural conclusion. You might feel calmer, or notice your posture relax, or let out a deep exhalation. These are your clues that something has been finished. This is how mammals feel once they have completed their escape from, and response to, a threat.

Then, from this new place, you can review the whole piece of work to find out what you need to do, when similar triggering situations come up.

Week Four, Day One
Boundary And Review

Now go back to the story you chose to work on from Day One of Week Two.

You're now going to finish this piece of work, creating a boundary from the work you began at that end of that process. Find the boundary prep from Day One of Week Two and write it out again.

It doesn't feel okay for me when ____

____

____

As you write this out again, and read it back to yourself, you might find that you have a different relationship with those words. When you first wrote them, they were an idea. Now they might be closer to a really clear instruction from your body. There is an expression "the body knows". When you feel it, you know what it means. Hopefully, you are getting a glimpse of that now.

From this new embodied place of deeper understanding of your needs, you are now going to make two new, vitally important statements. You are going to tell yourself:

What I need in the future

What I am going to do for myself to make sure I get it

You can figure out what you need in the future because it is related to what doesn't feel okay for you, as you stated in your boundary prep. If it doesn't feel okay for you to be shouted at, in the future you need to make sure that you don't get shouted at. This bit is usually that simple. The hard part is not making that someone else's problem.

If what I need is not to be shouted at, then I might think that this is something I need to persuade others to do for me. But then I've lost all of my power, when what I really need is exactly the opposite. That's why we need to take control of reducing the triggers in our lives ourselves.

Then ask, "What can I actually do for myself if the problem is being created by other people or situations" The answer is usually that we can do only two things. We can ask people to do things differently, explaining why, if we feel safe enough. Or if they can't, won't or don't, then we can choose not be around those people in these situations. That's it.

Ultimately, this might create some very difficult choices, like leaving a job or a relationship in extreme cases. But if that's what is necessary to rescue your nervous system, then it might well be worth it. Only you can decide. Going through this exercise of allowing the body to inform you about how it feels about the problem will help you know, deeply, what you really need. Usually, once someone knows this, nothing feels more important. The body knows.

If you can get this far, and have made clear to yourself and others what you need in the future, and are making sure that you get it, one way or another, you have reset the conditions for your world and made yourself more safe.

And once you are safer, your nervous system has more room to work with sensations, and, therefore, more chance of completing unfinished responses to earlier threats. If you keep going, it should get easier and easier.

So, what I need in future is ______________________________

____

____

____

____

And this is how I am going to take care of myself if I don't get ______________________________

____

____

____

____

See how that feels. Let it settle into your new nervous system. And breathe.

You have just completed one piece of work around one earlier threat in your life. If you want to, read back what you wrote on Day One of Weeks Two and Three. Then, read your boundaries above again.

Imagine what it would be like if you could do all of this automatically, the moment the trigger first happens. It's possible. That's your goal. It's what all this practice is for. Keep going. It will get easier.

Week Four, Day Two
Tracking Sensation

Today, we'll do the same again. Create a quiet space for yourself to do this work, and start with your favourite body scan video or audio recording.

After the body scan, read your time-travel from Day Two of Week Three. Read mindfully and slowly. Pay attention to your sensations and find one sensation that seems urgent. Then ask yourself:

Where is it?
What colour is it?
How big is it?
What shape is it?
What textile is it?
What temperature is it?

List the answers in your head. As you concentrate on your description of it, connect it to this sensation, and ask yourself:

And what happens next?

See if any of these qualities you've described change. Then, ask yourself this very important question:

Can you let that happen?

Let it happen until you feel a pause in the process.

Then, go back to the questions about the sensation:

Where is it?
What colour is it?
How big is it?
What shape is it?
What texture is it?
What temperature is it?

Then,

And what happens next?

See if any of these qualities change. Then, ask yourself:

Can you let that happen?

And then let it happen.

Keep going until you feel that things have come to a natural conclusion.

Week Four, Day Two
Boundary And Review

Go back to the story you chose as your main piece of work on Day Two, Week Two. Find the boundary at the end, and write it out again.

It doesn't feel okay for me when ____

____

____

Now that the body knows this, make two new, vitally important statements.

So, what I need in future is ____

____

____

And this is how I am going to take care of myself if I don't get it ____________________

____

____

See how that feels. Let it settle into your new nervous system. And breathe.

You have just completed one piece of work around an earlier threat in your life.

If you feel like it, read back what you wrote on Day Two of Weeks Two and Three. Then, read your boundaries above again.

Keep going.

Week Four, Day Three
Tracking Sensation

It's the same process again today. Have you settled into a rhythm for your quiet body scan yet?

After the body scan, read your time-travel from the same day last week, mindfully and slowly. Pay attention to your sensations, identifying one sensation that seems most urgent. Then, ask yourself:

Where is it?
What colour is it?
How big is it?
What shape is it?
What texture is it?
What temperature is it?

List the answers in your head, and as you concentrate on your description and connect it to this sensation, ask yourself:

And what happens next?

See if any of these qualities change. Then, ask yourself:

Can you let that happen?

Let it happen until you feel a pause in the process.

Then, go back to the questions about the sensation:

Where is it?
What colour is it?
How big is it?
What shape is it?
What texture is it?
What temperature is it?

Then ask yourself again:

And what happens next?

See if any of these qualities change. Then, ask yourself this very important question:

Can you let that happen?

And then let it happen.

Keep going until you feel that things have come to a natural conclusion.

Week Four, Day Three
Boundary And Review

Go back to the story you chose as your main piece to work on from Day Three of Week Two. Find the boundary at the end, and write it out again.

It doesn't feel okay for me when ____

____

____

Make two new, vitally important statements, helped by your body's wisdom.

So, what I need in future is ____

____

____

And this is how I am going to take care of myself if I don't get it ____________________

____

____

See how that feels. Let it settle into your new nervous system. Breathe.

You have just completed a further piece of work around an earlier threat in your life. If you like, you can read back what you wrote on Day Three of Weeks Two and Three.

Then, read your boundaries above again.

Keep going.

Week Four, Day Four
Tracking Sensation

Let's do it all over again. Is it starting to feel more natural yet? Don't worry if it isn't; it'll happen. After doing the body scan, read your time-travel from Day Four of Week Three mindfully and slowly. Pay attention to your sensations, pinpointing one sensation that seems urgent. Then ask yourself:

Where is it?
What colour is it?
How big is it?
What shape is it?
What texture is it?
What temperature is it?

List the answers in your head, and, as you concentrate on your description of it, connect it to this sensation, and ask yourself:

And what happens next?

See if any of these qualities change. Then ask:

Can you let that happen?

Let it happen until you feel a pause in the process.

Then, go back to the questions about the sensation:

Where is it?
What colour is it?
How big is it?
What shape is it?
What texture is it?
What temperature is it?

Ask yourself:

And what happens next?

Do any of these qualities change? Now ask:

Can you let that happen?

And then let it happen.

Keep going until you feel that things have come to a natural conclusion.

Week Four, Day Four
Boundary And Review

Go back to the story you chose as your main piece to work on from Day Four of Week Two. Find the boundary at the end and write it out again.

It doesn't feel okay for me when ____

____

____

Now make two vitally important statements.

So, what I need in future is ____

____

____

And this is how I am going to take care of myself if I don't get it ____________________

____

____

How does it feel? Let it settle into your new nervous system. Breathe and feel.

You have now completed another piece of work around an earlier threat in your life.

If you want to, read back what you wrote on Day Four of Weeks Two and Three, then read your boundaries above once more.

Keep going. You're making great strides.

Week Four, Day Five
Tracking Sensation

Last one! Work through the body scan, and then read your time-travel from Day Five of Week Three. By now, you'll be more used to getting back into the experiences your body was communicating to you and paying attention to your sensations. Find one sensation you'd like to focus on today. Then, ask yourself:

Where is it?
What colour is it?
How big is it?
What shape is it?
What texture is it?
What temperature is it?

List the answers in your head, and, as you concentrate on your description of it, connecting it to this sensation, ask yourself:

And what happens next?

Do these qualities change? Ask yourself this very important question:

Can you let that happen?

Let it happen until you feel a pause in the process.

Then, go back to the questions about the sensation:

Where is it?
What colour is it?
How big is it?
What shape is it?
What texture is it?
What temperature is it?

Then ask yourself:

And what happens next?

See if any of these qualities change. Then, ask yourself this very important question:

Can you let that happen?

And then let it happen.

Keep going until you feel that things have come to a natural conclusion.

Week Four, Day Five
Boundary And Review

Go back to the story you chose as your main piece to work on from Day Five of Week Two. Find the boundary at the end and write it out again.

It doesn't feel okay for me when ____

____

____

Now make these two important statements.

So, what I need in future is ____

____

____

And this is how I am going to take care of myself if I don't get it ____________________

____

____

How does it feel? As before, let it settle into your new nervous system.

You have now completed your fifth piece of work around earlier threats in your life.

Feel free to read back what you wrote on Day Five of Weeks Two and Three and your boundaries above again.

You are done!

Week Four, Day Six
Review

Wow. You've made it.

Congratulations on completing your 28-Day Plan. You've been through the whole process of retraining your thinking, human brain, reframing your life experiences, using what's left over to time-travel, and resolving where that took you back to.

One end result from this process in a boundary. Look back over the five boundaries you discovered this week, and reflect on what you have told yourself you need and what you have promised yourself you will do if you can't get it. You can't typically regulate your whole nervous system forever in one go, but you can start your own practice of boundaries in your life, which will keep you safer and make the work easier to continue.

I hope you have found some places in you that feel safer now and have good clues about how to adjust your life to make it safer, too. If you continue to combine these two elements of nervous system recovery, you should find that your life changes significantly for the better in the long run.

There will be many ups and downs because that's how the nervous system works, but you will find that, in time, the ups are better and more sustained and, the downs less far down and last less long, and that the swings between the one and the other happen less often

Welcome to a life an increasing regulation.

Give yourself a pat on the back.

You deserve it!

Week Four, Day Seven
Rest

Now let your system rest. Celebrate the beginning of the rest of your life.

Further Resources

Visit www.theinvisiblelion.com to find out more about The Invisible Lion and the resources which go with it, including treatment ideas, further reading, related publications, videos and blogs.

About the Author

Benjamin is the Founder of NeuralSolution, Khiron Clinics and Get Stable. He is also an accredited psychotherapist and entrepreneur. He has had a rich and varied career, combining his interests in psychology, the media and business. In his twenties he founded two small businesses before starting a family, training as a psychotherapist and writing his first book which led to presenting a television series for the BBC.

More recently he has combined his business experience, clinical training and media skills to set up Khiron Clinics, residential and out-patient mental-health clinics, to lobby for more effective treatment in the public sector through his non-profit Get Stable, and to found NeuralSolution which delivers nervous system informed technology for behavioural health problems.

You can find out more about his life and his work at www.benjaminfry.co.uk.

ANSWERS TO THE TEST

Day One	Day Two	Day Three	Day Four	Day Five
1 B	1 A	1 E	1 C	1 A
2 D	2 B	2 D	2 B	2 E
3 C	3 C	3 B	3 A	3 B
4 E	4 E	4 A	4 D	4 C
5 A	5 D	5 C	5 E	5 D
6 D	6 C	6 E	6 D	6 A
7 A	7 E	7 A	7 B	7 D
8 D	8 D	8 C	8 A	8 C
9 C	9 B	9 B	9 C	9 E
10 E	10 A	10 D	10 D	10 C

Printed in Great Britain
by Amazon

67677919R00046